Contained
David Turner

First edition published in 2019

Hesterglock Press
The Blue Room
25 Wathen Road,
Bristol
BS6 5BY
UK

Cover Design: Callum Beamon
Cover image: *Of Things I Can't Unthink* (plaster, nylon thread, 2016) by Carissa Baktay, photographed by D10photo

ISBN: 9781916159464

LOTTERY FUNDED | Supported using public funding by
ARTS COUNCIL ENGLAND

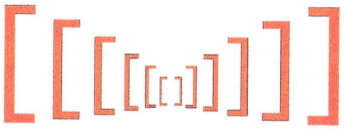

HESTERGLOCK PRESS

publish mostly the avant-garde / future-facing

With thanks to Elancharan Gunasekaran, who generously supports the work of Hesterglock Press and Paul Hawkins through Patreon, making this book & many others possible.

for information on all our publications and much more visit:

www.hesterglock.net
Twit: @h_g_press
Insta: hesterglock_press
E: hesterglock@gmail.com

David Turner is the founding editor of the Lunar Poetry Podcasts series, has a City & Guilds certificate in Bench Joinery along with the accompanying scars, is known to the Bristol, Kristiansand and Southwark Community Mental Health Teams as a 'service user' and has represented Norway in snow sculpting competitions. Widely unpublished. Working-class. Picket line poet.

lunarpoetrypodcasts.com
twitter.com/Silent_Tongue

for lizzy — everything

Contents

To listen to recordings of these poems scan the QR code below or follow this link:

www.soundcloud.com/david-turner-poetry/sets/contained

John Dickson

Raymond throws himself down next to me on the plastic two-seater sofa. With overuse the body of the seat gives, allowing us to slide into its heart. Track-suited thighs touching. As uncomfortable as this is, it is the least of our problems. *How did you sleep Raymond?* *They tried to fucking poison me again.* I've only been on the ward fifteen days and I've already had enough of Raymond's answer.
We sit in purgatory — we've had breakfast and medication but not the morning meeting — the day does not start without the morning meeting. Sit with track-suited thighs touching on plastic cushions watching the same twelve minutes and forty-five seconds of news do endless patronising forward-rolls on the wide-screen TV (behind scuffed Perspex) on the one wall that isn't covered with A4 sheets offering advice on mindfulness. A4 sheets daubed with spunking cocks, *fuck*, *fuck-off* and non-spunking cocks.
Lenny screams at Michael. In the twenty minutes since the nurses signed off confirmation that the tablets had been successfully transferred from the McDonald's ketchup pot to Michael's gut he had marched up and down both corridors around twenty-five times.
Paul is wanking in the corner. It's still only 08:49.
It occurs to me that it's in moments like this that the profound should deliver itself to me. Instead I turn to Raymond and say *it's alright, Jeremy Kyle'll be on soon.* As poisonous and claustrophobic as it is we rarely look out of the narrow, grated windows. Those locked doors don't keep us in, they keep our ghosts out. I try not to lose my shit over how one newsreader can no longer be trusted to read a story alone. In the courtyard a female patient screams something inaudible in the worst attempt at Jamaican patois prompting Raymond to shout *that lot downstairs are all fucking mental.*
We laugh in unison as the egg-timer is reset.

which comes about laughed at by hindsight / which burns cheeks, chills forehead, deafens ears/ which brings back *those* thoughts / which cancels plans and hides under duvets / which drinks to excess / which fightsfucks friends / which calls in sick / which *really* makes you go weak at the knees / which speeds heart rates / which tears at throats / which brings back *those* thoughts / which, tail between legs / which sheepishly / which… you are only animal after all / which reminds you of who you are / which lies / which lies / which lies / which happens in saunas / which happens in bedrooms / which happens on buses / which gets read out loud / which gets passed around class / which gets brought up *every* christmas / which happened last thursday / which you can write but never say / which when you're naked / which when they're naked / which they'd never forgive

Me and *G* were the only ones not to look at the wreckage

You claw at my flesh.   I make to go.
    Helpless.   Physically only the eyes stare back.
(Pink fat wedged under fingernails.)   Dulled irises the first sign.
And repetition doesn't ease the slide down.

You cling to meat — and to hope — and convince yourself this
won't be the temporary one. That this time I *will* be found.
Upturned and burned out in a Fenland ditch. Like the Vauxhall
Nova totalled by *that* lad with the eyebrow piercing.

Slowing alloy rims freewheeling in time with his fading heartbeat…
you're forced to watch as I head (blindly) off.   Out from
hollowed, charred sockets memories form trails of soot.

Flesh torn from bindings.   We become our own shadows.

And you'd cast your net over me — protect me from *this* — but I
already felt lost.   The best we can hope for is that more
often than not we're lost on the same path.

You insisted that you'd gladly follow (take the ride down with me).
But this is *reality* and you can't *just* be written into those scenarios.

Biscuits

They're still talking and you're not listening (what the fuck?). So, what's distracting you this time? Biscuits.   Fucking biscuits?   Well, not just biscuits but this idea — you know — how companies pay for advertising space in newspapers but lay the ad out to look like a story?   Like an article?   So, the (surely) non-existent *BBB* or *British Biscuit Board* might do this.   What were they talking about again? Job? You really should be paying attention. Something about lending. Or borrowing? They're still talking.   *If you don't dunk 'em, who will?* That'll be the 'headline' of the article/ad. It would vaguely encompass the idea that Britons are no longer dunking as much as they have in the past. Probably because we're all drinking artisanal coffee and you <u>cannot</u> dunk in a flat white. And there's this element of guilt because — you know — who will, if you won't?

Family? You're supposed to act interested, everyone knows that. Names? Birthdays? Parents? Alive?   Why biscuits? Why not trifle? They know you love trifle. You've already covered your, more-than-passing, interest in sploshing. Why not trifle? It's so creamy and welcoming. Biscuits are just dry and what you can do with a trifle —   They must have noticed by now, how could they not? You're doing that thing with your breathing again. Just breathe normally. In and out. That's all that's required.   You're not blinking properly. You're giving them an extra little squeeze at the end (or is it the beginning?) of the blink. Just be — you must look like you're trying to push your eyeballs back into your skull.

They just smiled. A joke? Are you supposed to laugh now? The only thing worse than not laughing at your date's joke is laughing at nothing.   Right, so if you ever needed proof that missing your medication three times in a week would cause problems, well here it is. Just like the good old days, eh? But, you know, you can't let tablets rule your life. And, how's that working out for you?   Michael Jackson?   The doctors at the Maudsley said to just be honest in these situations. So, what? You just come right out and tell them that you're not capable of following a simple conversation because you may become fixated on biscuits at any moment? Without judgement?   Peter Jackson? Films? You know nothing about films. How do you even know this guy's name? Charlie? Charlie talks about him a lot. Or maybe Kasper?   Ok, so just put your hands on the table, look them in the eye and tell them. You've forgotten to take your medication and it's affecting your concentration. It's not their fault.   They're still talking.

The Norwegian for gum translates directly as *tooth meat*

For months I found comfort in Cuntbarf's blog. Incessantly reading and re-reading her recipe for menstrual-blood cookies. Well, in between reading the internet's outraged reaction to the recipe. It's like they'd never seen an end-of-year Foundation Art show before.

I practiced by digging toothpicks into soft gums as I ate rich tea biscuits. The obsession with the recipe abated before I worked out how to collect my own blood.   But it never leaves you.

An early version of this poem was published on the *Blue of Noon* blog. I sent the link to Cuntbarf but never heard anything back.

She had a young son, a vegetable patch, a job in a diner and I'm sure not enough time to reply to 'poets' in south London.

I say *abated* but these things just get replaced by pushing / thumbing eyeballs back into their sockets or tapping forefingers against foreheads. As a kid I would push so hard I could see a greyscale brick wall and 'clouds'. Like falling down a '50s cartoon well.
        You tell yourself you enjoy these things.

In your late thirties your friends stop telling you stories about weekends on ketamine, instead it's how their kids' optician told them that rubbing your eyeball is the fastest way to glaucoma.

There's a loose consensus around the hummus and grown-up (expensive) crisps that obsessions are unconscious but this doesn't go any way to confronting how they don't ease up once they're pointed out to you.

Cuntbarf just stopped posting. Didn't say goodbye or delete her account. Just went and did something else.

There is probably a blog where her followers can come together and speculate about what happened to her — sub-sections of that blog divided into those who just think she got too busy, those who claim her son got to the age where he wanted his own online presence and the *hardcore* that have pieced together the posts and locations and want to visit the diner she worked at and demand answers.

The *rest of us* are left feeling uncomfortable with this sudden reversal in power.

████ told me recently about how mothers estranged from their grown-up children can be categorised into three groups online. (i) Those that admit they were the problem. (ii) Those whose child had issues that drove them away. But most tellingly (iii) those that are in denial that they were the problem. They go online and complain about their ungrateful offspring and their *terrible* spouses.

They *bleed* all over their keyboards and *the void* just laps it up.

Presumably the moderators know this is just good for business. I mean, we can't discuss this without admitting that maybe none of these people are who they say they are, that Cuntbarf may have just been a character.

A performance.

I've only heard of the 'estranged mothers' because of people assuming false identities just to watch these meltdowns. But Cuntbarf just looked so upset when she posted about the backlash toward the cookies — and the people I know logging into these forums are just looking for answers about some of the women in their lives.

I don't want to believe that Cuntbarf wasn't real but then I don't want to believe that I'm rubbing my eyes so hard that I can hear ringing in my ears.

Is it a problem if we all know it's false yet still get what we want?

There was a Domestos advert on the telly in the '80s and the noise that the *germs* made, sort-of-a-metallic-grinding-noise, haunted me for years and was the closest thing to what I 'heard' repeatedly as it felt like my brain scraped along the inside of my skull, but this is a useless point of reference if the psychiatric nurse taking the notes hasn't seen the advert.

It will remain a useless point of reference until you can find the ad on YouTube in a compilation of 'classic ads'.

And not finding it doesn't mean it hasn't been uploaded or that it never actually existed in the first place. It might just mean that you haven't gotten to grips with how search terms work.

Maybe you're just not very good at finding answers.

the teaspoon sets in motion / hot smooth steel scrapes against bone / first displacing then cupping my eye ball / the vibrations pass through cold fingertips / absorbed by your brittle knuckles / (tear duct detaches) / vision blinks out like the picture on my nan's timber-framed tv / metal connects with optical nerves / muscles instinctively (pointlessly) fight the extraction / milk falls in a narrow stream entering the centre of the whirlpool

the teaspoon sets in motion / hot smooth steel scrapes against bone / first displacing then cupping my eye ball / the vibrations pass through cold fingertips / absorbed by your brittle knuckles / (tear duct detaches) / vision blinks out like the picture on my nan's timber-framed tv / metal connects with optical nerves / muscles instinctively (pointlessly) fight the extraction / milk falls in a narrow stream entering the centre of the whirlpool

the teaspoon sets in motion / hot smooth steel scrapes against bone / first displacing then cupping my eye ball / the vibrations pass through cold fingertips / absorbed by your brittle knuckles / (tear duct detaches) / vision blinks out like the picture on my nan's timber-framed tv / metal connects with optical nerves / muscles instinctively (pointlessly) fight the extraction / milk falls in a narrow stream entering the centre of the whirlpool

the teaspoon sets in motion / hot smooth steel scrapes against bone / first displacing then cupping my eye ball / the vibrations pass through cold fingertips / absorbed by your brittle knuckles / (tear duct detaches) / vision blinks out like the picture on my nan's timber-framed tv / metal connects with optical nerves / muscles instinctively (pointlessly) fight the extraction / milk falls in a narrow stream entering the centre of the whirlpool

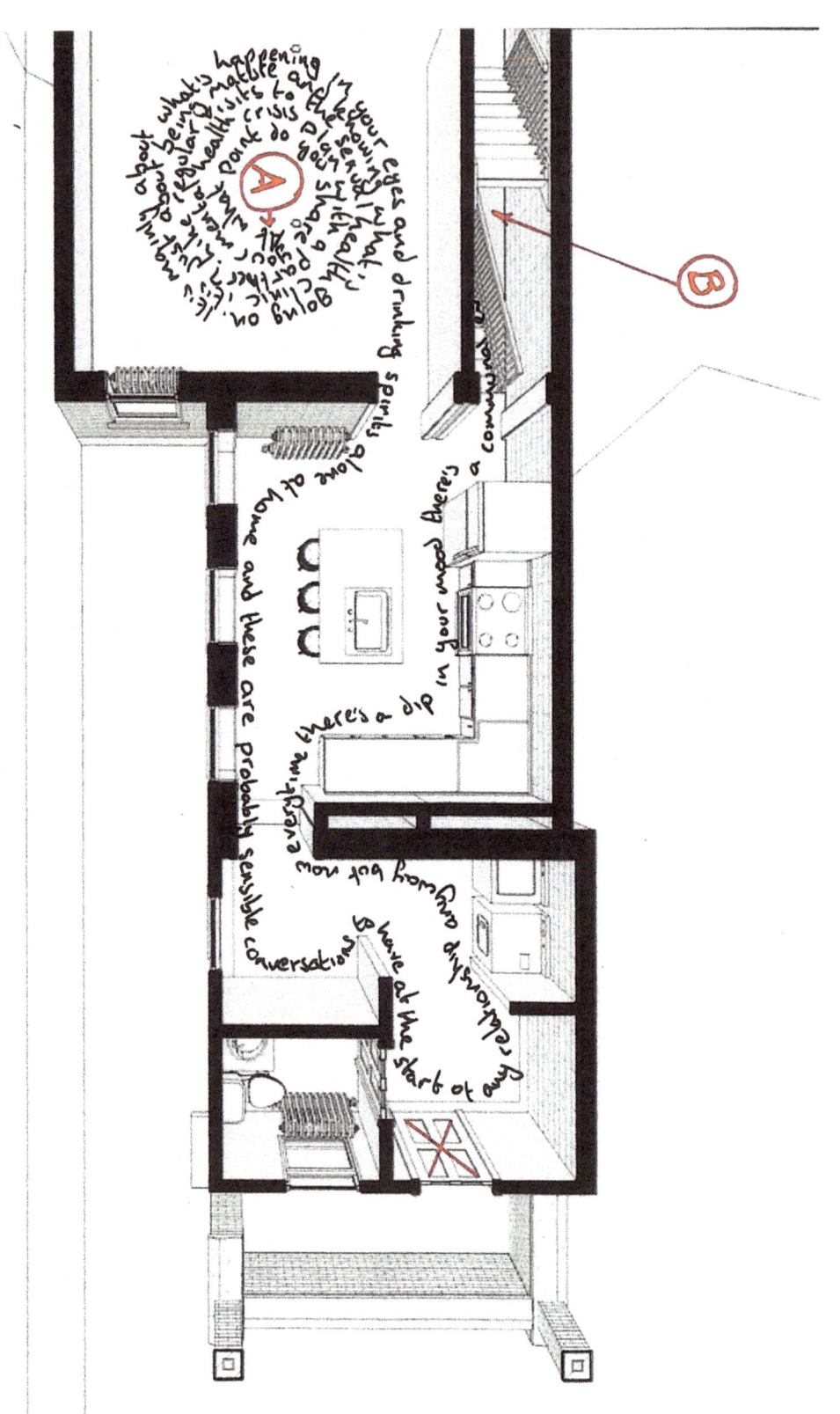

they don't call time while you're still drinking

You bit my cheek.
                    With searing-irons you branded my deceitful
flesh and I closed my eyes and hoped you'd devour me. Not for
overblown romantic reasons but because I'm a coward — because
feeling you shred me down to the bone was a more attractive option
than going home.

You told me how beautiful I looked with such full (swollen) lips and
I didn't tell you that I hadn't felt intimacy like that for too many
years.   The kind of intimacy that sinks its nails and teeth into you,
slams knuckles against cheekbones, sucks at soft flesh until it burns,
then praises the natural healing process.

                    Beautifies the swelling.

                                        How beautiful I am
with bloodshot eyes. And besides, we're dressed now so can forget
about my bruises, ignore how they seep into each other (yellowing)
and rut up against the next (deepening purple). An unspoken
acknowledgement that we're experiencing the same amount of pain
lay over us.

I stay silent as you jab at me with compliments, stay silent and replay
memories of east-Berlin bars which seemed to have opened decades
before just so we'd all have somewhere to meet.

The force of your bite promised that if I kept drinking, you'd keep
serving.

                    I'm the greediest person I know so drank us dry. I
don't think I ever told anyone how close I was to accepting your
invitation to stay, the coward in me wanted (more than anything) to
run away, the coward in me ensured I got on the plane *home*.

11

While on the John Dickson ward I was asked if I used the internet to engineer these recurring events, it seemed to be mistakenly read as arrogance when I answered that I could make this happen anywhere.   I've perfected the body language.

The look.

The lessons we're given to avoid *The Bad People* are the best guide to getting picked up.   I know how to get used and it builds stamina.

While friends were gurning (jaws rapid-cycling) as amphetamines tore along veins and fast-twitched through muscles I learned to be patient. Sometimes three days and nights of parties is *all* it takes to meet someone just as lonely.

Knowing your predator is the same as knowing your prey.

Because we're all hurting just as badly and I still can't explain why I feel like this is all I deserve and I cook because I want to please and I'll go down on you until my jaw locks because I want to please and I'll let you break my skin because I just want you to tell me I've been good. (In the moment, nothing else matters.) These sensations are all that matter.

Yet they ask about the past and I'd rather scratch my eyes out than discuss nature vs nurture. This endless debate doesn't answer why your teeth tearing at my flesh feels so_____

I don't need years of psychiatric experience to tell me why I'm so desperate to please.*

*No part of this acceptance gets me any closer to working out why I feel so, resolutely, that I don't feel like I deserve any better. I'm left wondering if I've ever truly cared about anyone or do I act in an attempt to feel part of something, a group or a family? Is the kindness I show just manipulation?

And I fucking despise the confessional because all I ever see is the worst of myself or worse still I see me. And I'm a coward. *They keep serving you this shit and you fucking lap it up.* But I write because we all know that damaged men find forgiveness through their art.

I seek redemption in order to repeat the same mistakes.

How is this misread as honesty?

What honesty is there in sharing selected highlights? Showing myself as weak or damaged? Waiting for you to tell me how my writing spoke to you so directly. Waiting for you to praise me.

The desperation is sickening.

I try to explain — I can never explain

Imagine a 1970s BBC documentary about the production of honeycomb. The bi-carbonated syrup expanding and rolling-ever-upward. No pan for containment. Now, picture the inside of my cranium. Threatening to swell over, collapsing with the release of steam. (Time freezing with my brain's inaction.) But this. This is just the come down. The early days. Body wrestling brain — treacle-footed, in the dull before the pills kick in.

Better this than the unwanted pre-psychotic dream space. Watching them file in again, and stand. (Why do they always just stand and stare?) Shoulder to shoulder at the foot of my bed. These men had once followed me in dreams, appeared on every rooftop, watched my every move around *Pimlico*. Paralysed me with terror through their inaction. It's always the memory of their eyes I'm trying to punch loose.

Starting before I'm fully awake.

I'd continue to punch until my knuckles softened. Bled. Trying to split open a temple. Allow the syrup to flow out freely. Carry in its stream their eyes and the insomnia. Eight days in now and my brain has started to solidify. Conform. But I still see their eyes. We blink them away together. Prolonged heavy, audible blinks. But it's only temporary.

rawl plugs are almost impossible to fill but
just make so much mess when ripped out

i brought tea (of course) and i'm still unsure what else
and we pretended (together) that the reversal of roles
wasn't really happening

at that age, watching them go to bed for six months is as
bad as three   and no one helps

these memories stick

no matter how hard you push them from your eyes
        block them out

misremembering often involves exaggerating any trauma
or sweeping it under the carpet   involves
getting bogged down in details

i watched you not watching the portable black and white
tv / not drinking the tea / not watching me

i ask if the process of trying to remember is a deliberate
protective act   protection from actually remembering
        and no one helps

i often forget the names of my cousins so maybe that's
just a part of me   perhaps i forget the names of
cousins and misremember flushing pills away

      and it burns   and i remember *everything* in bits
and it burns   and i remember the rage in *everything*
        and it burns

The weight of my knuckle on that eyelid rang through my ear canals like those French kids' screams in the (now back-filled) subway at *The Elephant*.

Blurred vision for what felt like days.

On occasion I've rubbed so hard I tore the skin.

Weigh-up your finger as substitute. (Definitely a better fit.) Your fingertip on the back of my eye. Knuckle against the socket for leverage.

You'll need to be sure though. Quick. I've always imagined there'd be a pop... alleviate the itching.

Hang the fucking thing in a net bag.
Watch the fucking thing dry out.
Swing the fucking thing round your head.
Smash the fucking thing against period architraves.
Soak the fucking thing in boiling water with
accompanying sachet of dried peas.
Throw the fucking thing off Waterloo Bridge.

As everything grows too big to comprehend throw the
fucking thing in *the drink*. It won't sink of course but
that isn't the same as floating (no part of me can float
unaided).

I'm too dense to float yet lack the common decency to
sink.

M (and everyone) asks me about the eyeballs

Every football hooligan's autobiography seems to contain a story about some poor fucker's eyeball getting sucked out of its socket. Knocked to the floor with a right hand or a lump of wood, some horrible cunt down on him with the misdirected kiss of life. Lips pressed on the eyelids. Suck. Pop. Out it comes. Easy as that… apparently.

But where's the satisfaction if the sound is muffled by the mouth? It seems too easy, too comfortable. In the films about these 'firms', the fella on the floor inevitably rolls around in agony but surely it's far more like something a cat would do to a kitten? — They lick their bellies to encourage them to shit, pick them up by the scruff to keep them out of danger and suck their eyeballs out to give them a wash? — There's no *actual* malice there. Surely the eyeball doesn't feel any pain? It's probably right at home there in the warm?

They should be called *eyelips* anyway.

I always think the directors are missing a trick here, where's the endoscopic camera view? The *horrible cunt* hasn't bitten the eyeball free so surely the *poor fucker* can see right down his throat? Pink, wet, pulsating sci-fi set. Alien world. And at what point does the one doing the sucking think, 'Well that's enough sucking. I have this fella's eyeball in my mouth now.' Rolling the orb around on his tongue, feeling the weight and the density of it. Letting it rest between his teeth.

It would probably be hard to concentrate on the chaos around them, sixty rival fans recreating a Stone Island-clad Guernica. As the noise of the crowd dulls and finally mutes he'll become intensely aware of how rough his tongue is against the surface of the eye, how it isn't perfectly round.

How with a delicate squeeze between his molars he can force the elliptical shape to further, elongate. (A pickled egg, that's what it's like.) Smooth enough to slide between his teeth and cheeks and soft enough to crush without much effort.

I don't know, maybe at this point he realises how intimate this violence is, how for a lot of men this is the closest they'll ever come to touching another man, taking them inside themselves? Feeling them on their tongue. Or he'll just continue to enjoy the sensation, and wonder why it doesn't taste saltier. But the eyeball doesn't cry, or feel, or even see. It just is. In his mouth.

Maybe the length of the optic nerve will surprise him? That and how he doesn't gag until something touches the back of his throat. As this all sinks in so does his full weight, through his hands, down onto the shoulders of him on the floor — mouth wide and presumably screaming. Fingertips dig into the fabric of a black Harrington jacket, gently kneading the muscle below. He feels like he's simultaneously swallowing him and falling into him, saliva building around the eyeball, he pictures his head as an egg. The eye the yolk, his spit the albumen, skull etc. and he's never felt any safer.

Pangs of guilt flash through the *horrible cunt's* conscience and he thinks about releasing but, you know, that'd be facing up to what you've done. Much better to stay still and endure the moment.

Taxis on Old Pye Street

I stand — ear toward the wind hoping to mimic your breath on
my neck.   Cars throw their lights.   Ignored they shatter on
wet concrete.

> Bleed out over tarmac.

The memory of your brittle cold fingers still pressed into my palm.

South of the river clouds are pulled to earth. Sucked into *the
Heygate's* exposed foundations.

> This beauty is a menace.

I (vaguely) recall telling you that an x-ray of my uncle's shoulder
looked like a crushed bag of crisps.

> You didn't flinch.

> We talk of destroying each other.
> Grinding those digits to dust.

Bus windows — blank canvasses.   Fur-lined parka hoods etch fine-
lines into condensation.   Hearts and arrows traced by fingertips.

> (Initials)

hers alone

I hadn't noticed the blood — sweating, my eyes were already burning. Richly oxygenated, the *claret* ran freely. Under lime-scaled shower heads we wiped my blood from each other. You tried to reassure me. (I tried to rid you of me.) Halogen spots throw at ceramic-tiled walls through cascading droplets. Shattered they illuminate my skin.   (Blue neoprene.)   You misread my embarrassment. What with, what just happened in there with you (and them).

I position my hands to protect my most intimate parts. Right hand covers the slug of a scar formed after the baseball bat nipped open the fragile skin stretched over my razor blade of a hip bone. (Skin peels back as you tap fingernail on brittle bone. (Pause to appreciate the sound I make (Push the finger into the wound. (Hook into position. (Threaten to snap free a trophy.)))).) Left hand over right shoulder. These contours are not for you to know. *This is for her.*

Clavicles popped inward by her rigid thumbs. Arms dropping. Gaze held. You can. You have had the rest. But these are hers alone.

String-section
After Sturmgeist by Erik Pirolt

To vibrate through every nerve. Resound in all of me(you). Your music in me(us). I am us now.

Femur scratches across arterial vein. I offer parts for you to strike. Offer parts for you to crush.

I hoped that the urge to pop eyeballs would disappear, the gobstopper now merely sits between your finger and thumb. Blood, the tears mapping unseen valleys and ridges (played/players/play).

You don't cry through fear but because you understand; you know that this all   makes   sense — that these are the only rational thoughts I have.

To be plucked out and crushed. Destroyed under the weight of (be)longing.

(and I always panicked when my lungs caught on splintered ribs and now take comfort knowing those splinters always were your finger nails, picking at the carrion)

You claim to be immune to that poison but we both know you don't want that to be true. This won't be how we go. (Shame.)

We don't wait for that someone to come along and save us. We wait for them because they understand how quickly this needs to end.

everybody is always very supportive / rubbing my arm and maintaining eye contact as they tell me how well i'm coping with everything / how people like me are an inspiration and constant reminder of how much more difficult their lives could be / genuine in their claim that i can call them anytime i'm feeling down / that the diagnosis must have come as a relief / that three tablets a day is *nothing really* / how confident they are that with time i'll *beat this* //// until i tell them about the incident with the axe

Sharky & George vs some anime thing

Over roast potatoes and brussels sprouts (no crackers (Christmas, not cream)) we give examples of how our Instagram feeds advertise to us the products we were talking about in front of the '24hr Music Channel' (Christmas hits (hits (hits))) before *literally* asking Alexa to beatbox along to Mariah Carey.   These devices listen to us and it's only okay when they're doing as they're told.   And you politely nod and indicate that you really liked the asparagus (you have not tried the asparagus) and you continue to politely nod and agree with your aunt (dad's side) that Christmas trees are far better decorated randomly and in a couple of weeks you'll politely nod and insist to your aunt (mum's side) that it's really nice to colour coordinate.

And you're sure Instagram knows that you're in bed and won't be venturing out in the rain for Kit-Kats but taunts you anyway. The Guardian advertising banner is clearly fucking *on one* in thinking that you were googling Bösendorfer pianos with the intention to buy and not to just feel morally superior (or jealous (definitely jealous)) over anyone that can spunk £140,000 on a music box.   Too many cookies will make you sick.   I refused to get an Oyster card because I didn't want it to know where I'd been but pay no mind to that Feeld app knowing *everything else*.

My sibling (2000).   Me (1981).   I've aged well so have to resort to the cliché of joking about being *soooooooooo* much older but the deeper you dig the clearer it becomes that the only difference between us is the method *they* use to extract money from our bank accounts. And the cartoons we remember — which is sort of the same thing.

Camberwell

We walk into the shopping centre (the one down at *The Green,* yeah? ((with the two bus stops next to each other)) (((where the McDonald's is))) ((((*they* call it a shopping centre but it's actually just a roof over a walkway — not really wide enough to be an *Arcade*)))) opposite Greggs). Like a greyhound out of the traps (remind me to tell you about my nights spent, trackside, at Wimbledon), this security guard rushes over, smiling, like. Only, she's not a security guard. (The nametag suggests honesty, assuages fears we didn't know we have or even need.) She's offering/selling insurance or the enigma that is Fibre-optic Broadband (Alan never understood the *concept* of broadband ((even when I employed the plumbing analogy)) (((*three-quarter* versus *'alf-inch*))) I can see now it's not the same thing). And I, of course, assume she's lonely, like the rest of us but we've become so sceptical, so distrusting. *Harvesting your data,* that's how *they* put it. (But I can't get credit when *I'm* me, how can they do it when *they're* me?) And it was her outfit that confused us, too sombre to sell the one-month-free-trial. (Because if you *really* think about it, like, whenever you see a butcher and think *his apron/coat-thing is very clean, he must be on his way to work* but then you notice he's wearing a hat and, like, you're sure it's only fishmongers that wear hats.) It just goes to show how important appearances are.

Sounding

after "Vibrert rom gråter ikke" by Erik Pirolt

You questioned whether I actually, truly feel anything (diary entry — 6/8/2015). You asked (yourself) if my heart was the same as others. You suggested (patronisingly) that, anatomically at least, the chambers and sinews inside our hearts would mirror each other. You claimed (arrogantly) that what I'm missing is the same capacity as you to hold and feel those emotions.

So, I've been thinking about my friend's fetish. The one who likes to slide tuning rods into his urethra (He says that you can't knock the idea until you've tried it. (Though, he says that about *all* of his fetishes.).) The rod carries the vibrations deep into his pelvis. Below the nerve endings which would normally process these sensations.

    I've been thinking…   All I need to do is push one of these rods between these two ribs *here* into my left ventricle and you'll be able to see, above the surface, what I'm feeling underneath.

I've been thinking that.

Phosphate of calcium
after John Berger

Your fingers
splayed pinions, reach
and rest upon me and
I feign discomfort, try
to wriggle free but I'd be
lost without that *dried-slip-thin*
touch… phosphate of calcium
is just dust. We
are just dust. Clavicles—
sticks of chalk —
pop, not snap (burst of
powder) — Miss Haversham's
reception spread. We'd
do lines of each other,
big fat party lines,
greedy to consume. Phosphate
of calcium is just dust.
We are just dust.
(Firn has the look of glacial
ice but like grains of sand
only holds together under
compression) *Bone china*
explodes at the right pitch,
gilings escape their
form. Once exposed to
the heat of the kiln nothing
is ever the same again —
phosphate of calcium is
just dust — after the kiln,
becomes ash, carries
our nostalgia, *keeps safe.*
We are just dust.

Tetris

And your bills will be split between four. And we can just draw up a rota for the oven. And you'll be sharing with creatives. And all the cleaning products are included. And this is one of the *better* parts of Peckham. And the room overlooks an impending park. And no DSS (Sorry, agent's stipulation. Not ours). And Elephant & Castle is becoming *so* vibrant. And there's no living room. And agent's fees apply. And Borough Market is just a bus ride away. And the breakfast bar seats two (three at a push). And we all respect each other's privacy. And you'll get your own cupboard in the kitchen. And no couples (Sorry, agent's stipulation. Not ours). And it would suit someone working nights. And you'd be sharing the bed with two Italian guys. *AND IT'S A SUPER FUN AREA WITH GREAT TRAVEL CONNECTIONS!* And there's a futon in the kitchen. And it's a great deal because the landlord isn't supposed to be sub-letting. And we're all recent graduates. And we all work in the city. And we're two gay guys. And we're three single women. And the room would suit someone similar. And there's a coffee shop that does an *amazing* flat white on the same street. And sorry but no working from home. And I'm only leaving the flat because I've got the chance to travel around Asia. And this is not a party house. And you'll be close to some great galleries and bars. And this is the perfect location to explore London from (zone 6). And no loud sex noises please. And we're all really sociable. And that's why there's a fold-down table in your bedroom for meal times.

EAT DA RICH

My poem 'Tetris' got commended in a competition by (famous) poet Luke Kennard (I get asked a lot "do you have any famous poets on your podcast?" I always reply "famous for poets" (there's a look I've become accustomed to that implies "I meant *famous* famous" (what am I supposed to say?))).   I choose the *cool poet* option (second of the two available) and do not include "…his poem 'Tetris' was commended by Luke Kennard…" in my writer's bio.

I've tried to distance myself from the poem but it's a rare object that can fit neatly on a page or in a column in the Morning Star (solidarity comrades!).   The *game of Tetris* I wanted to talk about was never the one that slotted neatly together. (Satisfying (Neat.).) It was supposed to be the game that was clearly fucked only half way up/down the screen. You're now rapidly/randomly hitting $\Downarrow$, $\Rightarrow$ and $\Leftarrow$ to just get through it and start again. Piling blocks wherever they fall revealing pockets of (potential)   air   around the screen.

That's me on the bottom row trapped in a shared house just off Camberwell New Road. Contained by a fourth-hand (Ikea) double mattress and housing benefit that falls 150 notes short of my rent each month.   It divides Britain (apparently) whether or not we deserve social housing. Those of us whose dad had two aunts in the flats on Wyndham Road — whose nan and grandad got married in St. Mark's church at the Oval — family at the top of the Walworth Road — on low or no incomes — unable to work more than temporarily, either for short periods or longer.   I used to always try and use the phrase *London Stock* (bricks, mate) in poems but poets are conditioned to be terrified of clichés so I did the decent thing and supressed that urge. They're there for a reason though.

I sometimes think it's just a big laugh on the part of The Right to persecute poets. They know that those of us on the other side of the overly simplified binary divide will all rally around and focus our time on this ineffectual nonsense. The Tories are masters at maintaining a collective numbness until we reach a point and explode and can ultimately be painted as unreasonable.

My favourite railway/canal graffiti has always been **EAT DA RICH** but tbh I'm struggling enough with gluten.

Generations brought to London to do the dirty / dusty / dangerous shit. Housed in brick tenements and well-meant concrete blocks working in power stations, caffs and garages in railway arches. The Heygate Estate has now been replaced by glass, steel and 24-hr concierge services and parts of The Aylesbury still stand empty after the *decanting* of hundreds of families.   One of the most bitter aspects of this gentrification is that it's always at its most extreme in areas with Labour councils and MPs. We've had our communities sold out from under us by the same people offering to put their arm around our shoulder.   From Orgreave ⇒ Hillsborough ⇒ Grenfell, neglect from the state toward the working class (passive or otherwise) is never publicly acknowledged as criminal.   Anything that happens to us is just an unfortunate consequence of our surroundings.

now fuck off please, we'd like to sell sourdough on Deptford High Street

██ hadn't been in London long when he asked if I'd show him around Brixton. I don't normally indulge that sort of behaviour but I understood what he meant by wanting to see the *real London*. I thought the cabbie had dropped us off in Clapham until I saw The Ritzy sign (give Picturehouse cinemas a swerve for treating their staff like shit and not recognising unions). I had only been out of the country a few years but the place had been turned upside down. Now, my nan was mugged twice in broad daylight in Brixton Market when I was a kid and there's no denying the area needed to be made safer for everyone living there but there has to be an intermediate point between old women being robbed and Franco Manca.

> Between a near-constant (perceived) threat of
> violence and communities being dismantled.

█ slice of
stainless-steel teeth
█ optic nerves
through █
█

apprehensively you
█ the olive
grabber into my ear
canal i nod
encouragement as
█ break the
paper-█
resistance of the
ear drum you ask
how you'll know
when to stop you'll
just have to dig
deeper █ the
tool tearing flesh i
pat your █ in
reassurance as
█ pools before
tracing my jawline

one poem about sex and that's it ok

It isn't clean and we don't want it in our mouths. Returned pint glass with lipstick on the rim. We'll drink any old piss before we'll ask for a fresh drink but draw the line here.

You wake up in horror on the Northern Line at Kennington realising you've been resting your head on the day's accumulated grease. The glass dividers are supposed to keep us apart and we don't want any trace of the others lingering on us.

Walking through the vaper's *sweetshop mist* is somehow worse than the traditional smoker because it's mainly their breath, innit? They've entered you. Even though you've expelled all trace of them it's sort of their memory hanging around. Clinging to your insides.

You're sitting in one of those rigid plastic chairs in Café House Restaurant (*the* caff) on the Walworth Road and it's still warm and you'd move but you've been fixated on your nan's disapproving look (it only takes a look) for just long enough that someone would definitely notice you moving. Like a heat shadow.

As financially challenged teenagers we'd share bottles of MD 20/20. Our biggest fear between the ages of 12 and 16 seemed to be *backwash*. All this energy spent trying to avoid the 'wrong person's' saliva getting in your mouth.

Creased green slips

(1) — I read the word 'fluoxetine' in Claudia Rankine's *Don't Let Me Be Lonely* and can't remember actually having swallowed that particular poison but I do still remember the parts of me removed. The parts of me dissolved by this and other prescription drugs. The metallic taste they warn you about is just regret. The end of taste. You go along with the idea that psoriasis and tremors are better than what came before but they don't read your notes, especially the bit about wanting to please everyone. And it isn't ironic that the lithium keeps you alive while slowly poisoning you — it's the most beautiful and pure thing you'll ever experience. So perfect you just want to stop.

(2) — ▉▉▉ went to ▉▉▉▉▉▉ for the weekend I was first prescribed Abilify. All of our friends were jealous of our flat above an old corner shop. It didn't feel that desirable as I twitched and sweated for hours on a double mattress on a dusty wooden floor. There's nothing quite like feeling the moment that capsule dissolves and releases into your gut. Cue the shit.

(3) — The first ten days was just sleeping pills. On the ward we queued morning and evening outside the examination room and waited for our tablets/eye contact. The broom cupboard had been transformed into the examination room which was transformed into a dispensary by closing the bottom half of a stable door. The bottom section was lipped with a pale hardwood, bulging out in the middle to form a shelf, itself recessed like a soap dish. ██████ rejected Catholicism before I was ████ so I have no working knowledge of communion but all of the rage.

(4) — In the ███████ café my back spasmed so hard and so relentlessly I thought I might have to ask ███████ to hold me up. She (naturally?) assumed that my distraction was boredom (again?) and I had to apologise for her frustration as the layers of flesh on my back slid, one over the other. I hadn't even considered it might be a date until her lover 'accused' us and I found myself having to apologise when all I wanted to say was that I liked her boyfriend far too much to ever do that. But I'm *ethically non-monogamous* and none of it bothers me anyway and could they maybe give me some space as my kidneys and spine attempt to reject me.

(5) — At 11 ▮▮▮ asks you to flush away prescription medication. Too young to realise that working-class women are all too often just given something to shut them up. Not too young to realise that you shouldn't really have anything to do with this process. Knowing nothing about sedation or addiction (or proper sadness) you sit on the edge of the bed wondering when they'll ever wake up. 15" black & white tv on faux mahogany dressing table. Regional ITV showing football results — everything could have been so different (for so many people) if Cambridge United had progressed through past the playoffs. Dion Dublin → Manchester United → Homes Under The Hammer. It was the only peace the house ever experienced and I still can't remember where ▮▮▮ was when all this was happening and this might be my greatest source of shame.

(6) — At first Quetiapine felt like *the one*. Sleeping too much felt like a novelty. Mistiming the evening's dose and the next morning was all *buffering* into the streets of Kristiansand/Southwark. The question remains, at what point does machinery become too heavy to operate? At what point does your brain become too heavy to operate? But you're sleeping so much there's no time to complain to your doctor so everyone's a winner right?

(7) — The bloods clinic at Guy's Hospital was directly above (or below) the sexual health clinic. Two birds with one stone. The lithium would, supposedly, supress my libido but the sudden freedom from a lot of the self-loathing seemed to have the opposite effect. I've never been so aware of my own body. The phlebotomist apologises for making you wait. You apologise for carrying a bag and wearing too many layers. They apologise for any potential discomfort. You apologise for not being able to hold your arm out properly at that angle. They apologise, in advance, in case you end up with a bruise. You reassure them that this is your life now (three-month cycles) and of course apologise for taking up so much of their time.

(8) — ■ asked me if I identify as having a disability. I didn't have space to text back that all I could truly say is that I've been disabled. Like I only identify as a writer when writing. (All too often poetry makes you feel like a cunt.) There are no defined holes to point to when they inevitably ask you to explain. It's more a slow and sustained erosion. I mean, you tell people you feel hollow and clasp your abdomen/chest but really you just feel less than. Simultaneously lighter and heavier. I grew up hearing distressed or traumatised people talked of as being *in bits* and we laugh about it now but when my wife and I first met, every spilled coffee, every involuntary outburst, each alarm to take my medication was all just a backdrop to me trying to find all the bits of me scattered around South London. As crass as this may be, I've always likened it (in my head (only)) to the landing scene in Saving Private Ryan where the soldier is carrying his arm. Obviously comforted by having it back but completely baffled as to how the fuck it ended up on the floor in the first place.

your eyes is wet — i want to lick them (a recipe for making fudge)
after Gunmetal (for Ian E) by Rishi Dastidar

The sky is just fucking awesome, ok, and doesn't need a weapons-based simile to make it so

your eyes — as if drawn by hanna or barbera — always half empty. the

high tide measured against the soft-crack of your iris. the hard-crack of your pupil. sky-

ward. resistance is

measured against temptation. *just*

dip a finger. salty-sweet (reassuring sting).   and we waste time on poetry instead of facing up to how we're not fucking.

      the norwegian kids watched — in awe —

as i beat evaporated milk into sugar syrup. i constantly pour energy into this shit and it always (eventually) makes me sick. i don't do *some.*

how do we measure ok?

and

42

we've been lied to.   it doesn't

get easier. it just becomes the norm.   you don't
need

me in the way that you believe but you have me and this is the
beauty we'll never write. it's *our* truth. a

version of it anyway.   your damp looks create the incisions from
which the whole mess flows.   and here's the thing, right? there's
no filter to separate the pain from the beauty   the pretentious cunt
from the newly wed. (and poetry's not helping.) and i talk about
your eyes like knives (ffs!).   a weapons-based

simile!

the more air you incorporate into

the syrup, the harder it is to work. the air is the difference between
toffee and fudge. both sickly sweet but one more likely to rip out a
filling.   we push hard to make

space for the air but there's no filter. a void is just there to be
filled. if you're not paying attention, what flows back fastest is the
shit...

so

Rim

In week three we're tasked with writing a self-portrait. *Expose yourself to a mirror.* But it's #2018 and most people I know only need to scroll through the photo gallery on their phone (we wait for upgrades ((wish our contracts away)), every 18-months brings improved resolution on each pubic hair). Digital pocket-mirrors, mistakenly, reveal all to the old girls on the bus / Italian students on the tube / unsuspecting English teacher by the avocados in Tesco. We send reminders to each other from the warmth of the laundrette or to the tune of rattling china (jumping at us from tiled walls) down the caff and further up (the) Walworth Road the reflection of our skin (in the window of the Brazilian butcher) redresses the bare kidneys on stainless steel trays. (The steel cut with scouring pads, the blood of various ((two)) animals filling the troughs, as the grime and grease of our lives ((transfers from fingertips)) backfills the scratches on our screen protectors and *vaselines* our image.)

— foetal, my breath filters through your hair, sensation drains from the arm that bears the weight of your cycling chest and we're safe enough for me to whisper how fearful i am of this safety, damp contact as you tuck into me, hot/moist is the near-vacuum between our skin, the creases in the bedsheets cut contours —

I've had years of practice but still hate the sight of my body at arm's length, I'm only ever properly framed through my wife's lens and now (then) I've given up drinking I no longer need to peel the skin of my wrist away from sticky pub tables and only a poet would ever tell you that true beauty exists in this tension (for poet read *prick*). And I write because I can't paint and tell myself that I can't paint because I don't have the patience to draw and the pen makes for a shit knife anyway. It'll never expose what's important, how it all needs cutting out. (Cauterized, the truth smells like pork scratchings.) We don't write about our skin (not now there's ((was)) a Tumblr account) and sometimes I think we dismiss our eyes for *only* seeing reality.

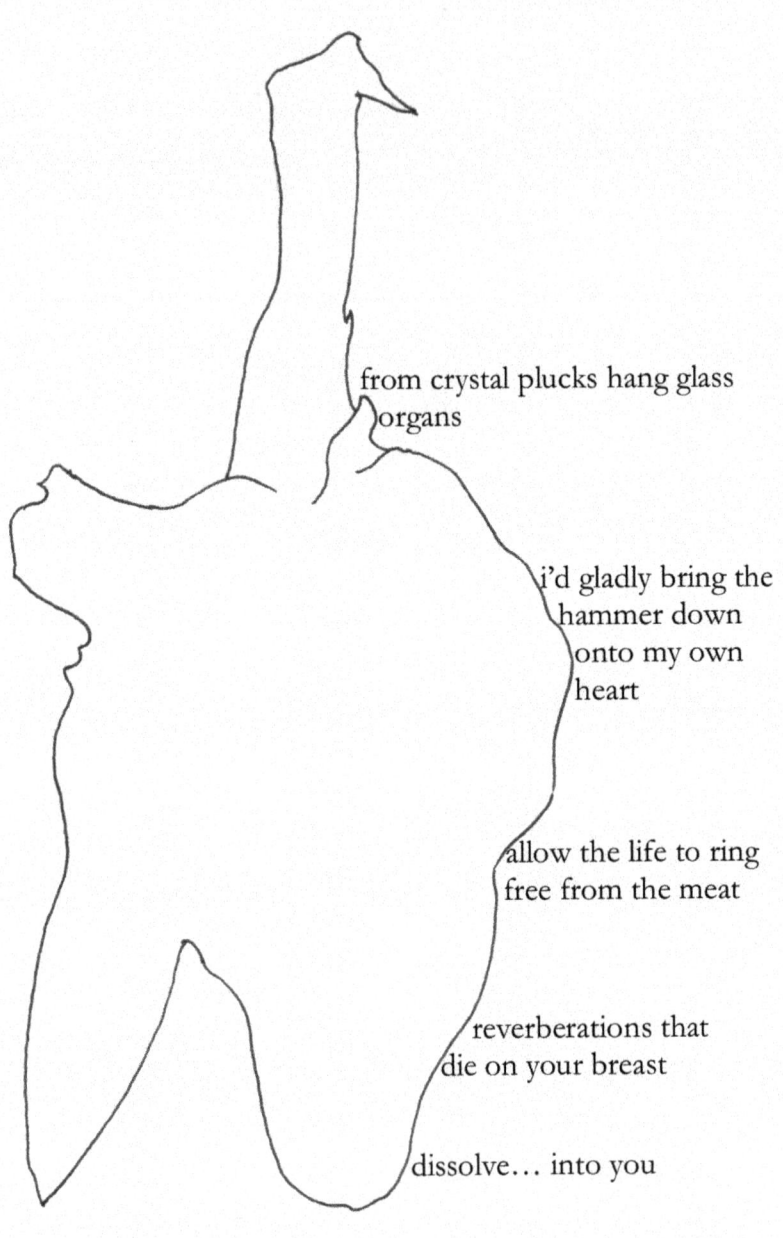

from crystal plucks hang glass
organs

i'd gladly bring the
hammer down
onto my own
heart

allow the life to ring
free from the meat

reverberations that
die on your breast

dissolve... into you

Kerf
after Riot Break by Erik Pirolt

this gift for you
                              this torn skin
          this muffled-clack of saw teeth skipping over radius
                         these vibrations through worn-out-oak-table-top
                                             these hairs on neck
          this burn of rising sick
                                   this involuntary finger
                    those snapping tendons
this skin already drained white
                         pop of tension released from marrow
bone, blade not honed for flesh, absence of any doubt that this act
could win your heart   that dream sequence of us
walking (that) hand in hand(s) those times i pressed blades into my
flesh   that i'm proud to do it for you (empty gesture for them)
               that will (should) change now   these weren't
empty promises   there just *aren't* the words   this
reality
          that *my* reality is that *this* is relief
                              i wait for you to hold the limb and me

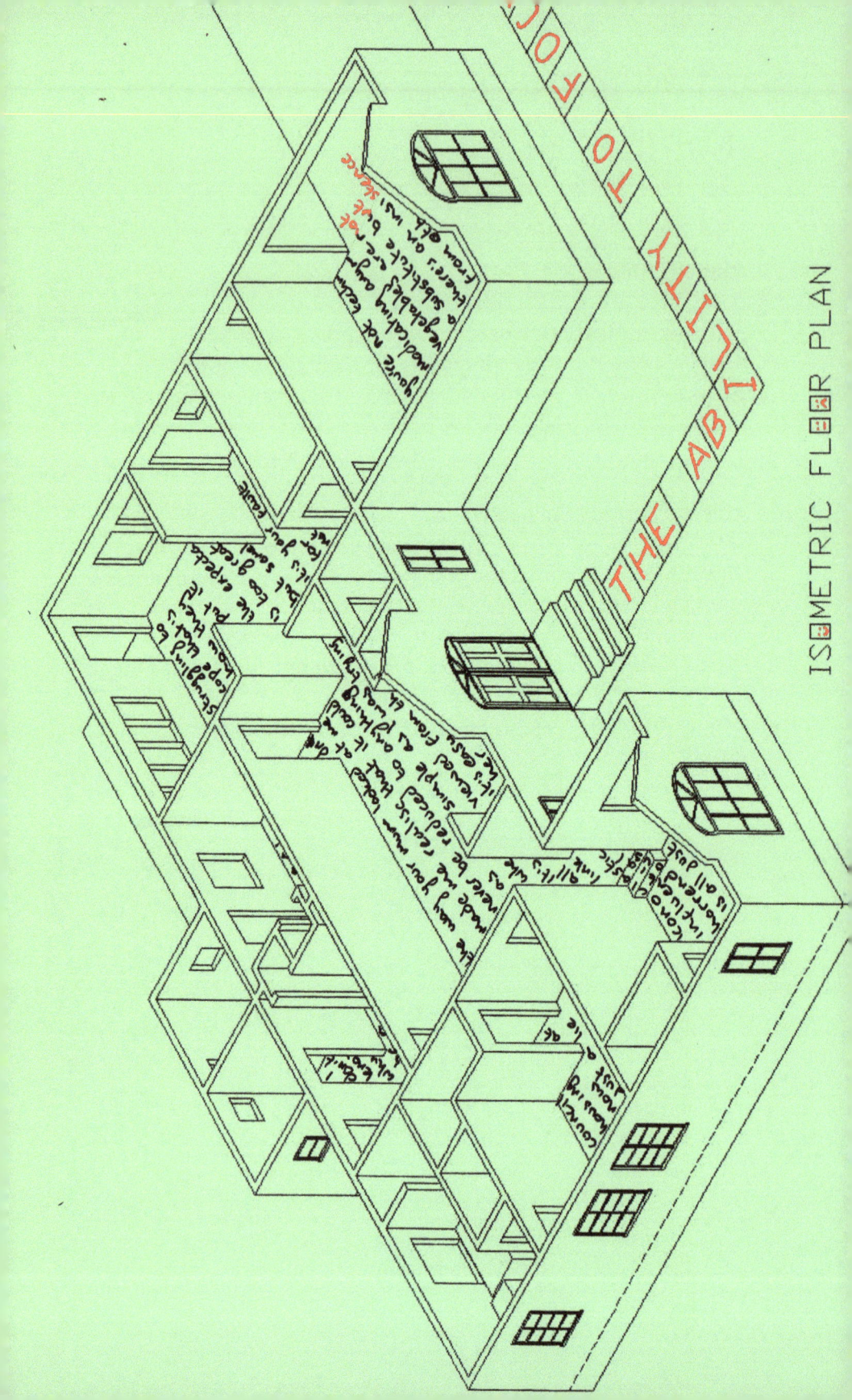

ISOMETRIC FLOOR PLAN

May 31st 2017
for lizzy

Mine is a wife that has lived my funeral. Over. And over. Re-runs interspersed with mealtimes and commutes.

Hers is a husband that runs from himself. Leaves her behind. Hides from the shame.

Ours is a happiness saturated by fear.

> We don't write about our wedding day. Not each other or our friends. We don't write about the contradiction of standing in front of you all and promising ourselves, only, to each other.
>
> Or how — no matter how much we love you all, none of you mattered. How we'd have gone through with it on *any other* Wednesday on Peckham Road.
>
> We don't write about our wedding day because our words don't match the *Instagram* accounts.

Mine is convinced all of this is going to be stolen from her.

Hers is panicked by the word.

Ours is a life of eulogies rehearsed, under shortened breath in preparation.

Deadline Day

That's the word they always use. *Cathartic.* As if any of this actually makes you feel any better. These ideas do not come to rest gently in your nut. They're mosquitoes steaming into the backs of your eyes. Why begin when you're just a few lines (a few hundred words (a page away)) from proving you're wasting your time?*

* Harry Redknapp's face melts through my headphones.

Like Armando Iannucci says about satire being dead because reality is already *too* ridiculous.

Harry's *boat* is beyond metaphor.

Wait.　　Not *actually* mosquitoes.　　So, these ideas are a gobstopper which you can *just* get between your teeth but it's — it's too hard to bite into / Your jaw just won't budge / But you've got hold of this idea and you're drooling but at the same time your teeth and gums are drying out / You're thinking that now you've got hold of this idea, "I don't want to let this go"/ But everyone's looking at you and laughing because you're drooling and your Adam's Apple is snapping up and down and you're like, "if I can just break into this I'm going to feel a lot better" / Though the reality is that you're just going to mangle the lot in order to get it to fit comfortably in your mouth.　　While drooling.　　Cathartic? / What part of *no* do you not understand? / Because poems don't stop you from falling (jumping) / Prescription medications kill / Kill / Kill / Preserve.

And metaphors can fuck *right off.*   They only exist so that when the person you love asks, with a smirk, if you were writing about them, you have an escape route.   A place to hide.
     Catharsis?

Being published in *The Dizziness of Freedom* was an amazing way to engage with writers that understand, on a base level, what I'm writing about but I'd really just like some time to myself to work things through

You can simultaneously be pleased (grateful even) that your wife was offered the CBT course and jealous that all you have is the creased green slip of a repeat prescription. You can. But you can't talk about it. You can't talk about it after your (latest) discharge from 'The Community Mental Health Team'. You can't talk about it since you've found the optimal dosage of the latest of a (long old) list of mood stabilisers. 300mg allows you to sleep and seemingly not much else (and you do/don't acknowledge that at the time of writing those blister packs have remained untouched for weeks). And you can simultaneously feel better and so much fucking worse, but you can't talk about it because there's just nothing for scale — *Okay, one last time. These are small, but the ones out there are far away.* — And we measure our success by not letting blood or jumping out of the window or going up to that bridge that hangs over this city that will never be home. We are left to measure our own success after being constantly reminded that we're worst placed to see it. Even Fabian knows that. And we can't talk about it because talking is *only one of the options available to us.* An option obscured by Quetiapine (well, this time). We've got nothing for scale.   And every single mental health professional I've come into contact with has raised the spectre of *unrealistic expectations* (even Fabian), but I don't see how it's unrealistic to assume we might *explore all the options available to us* and why no one ever mentioned that I might need to prepare myself for feeling bitter toward my wife.

Again

I cried at breakfast.   The sadness rose from the kerbstones on Carter Street. Up through damp and crumbling London-stock. Through joists and lino. Through mouse carcasses and greening copper pipes. And found me. Again.   And the choice is simple. Puke or cry.   But I've never been able to make myself sick and your face becomes theirs.   And at the same time you are *K*. And at the same time you are *E*. And at the same time you are *R*.

But I'm still me and I'm still crying at breakfast.

Because there are times when there is just no escape. You don't escape yourself and I was there in Berlin and I was there in Stockholm and I was there in Chicago and I'll never find the words to say that their faces wash over yours.

As my tears fall onto fried eggs, my eyes flick over to the window. We're three storeys up and it would probably work. (I focus again on the plate.) If I misjudged the fall, I'd just be gifting you an even more distant version of me. And I try to push wet egg-whites past my swollen tongue. And the tears still fall and the sound is winding down.   You lay a damp, warm palm on my arm in a way that whispers, *it will all be fine*. In a way that screams *I want this to stop*.   And in their faces your eyes remain — perennially damp and alone.   And we both know the window is an option.

Our attraction to this idea of *one final romantic gesture* is the risk we feed and nurture and we joke about how they're all waiting for me to do this. Prove them right.

And I'm desperate to speak and tell you that my biggest fear in these moments is that the tears will never stop and that the dormant sadness will gain control. And how after months of anguish you (still wearing a combination of all of their faces) will break. The ambulance — lightless and silent — will stand waiting for me.   You, held back by familiar palms that whisper *he'll be fine* and scream *this had to stop*.

And I'm still crying and you radiate love and it overwhelms (and so often makes this worse). And your damp eyes insist that crying forever is a better option than the window. And that you, at least, won't be the one to call for the ambulance.

The Crystal Dome is/isn't universal enough an image to hang a poem from

A disembodied finger starts the fan suddenly (there's a cane somewhere), and fucks the gold and silver fragments of my life (all-a-glitter) around the inside of the prism. The obviously-titled tickets (#publication, #rest, #contentment) immediately stick to the glass and remain out of reach. The rest (#job, #ACE-funding, #intimacy) taunt me — lash out at my eyelids, slap the back of my neck [in the following line I liken plastic-foil tickets to fish — and I'm sorry] The *pikelets* slipping through my fingers. *The World's Shittest Snow Globe*™.

The boot on my chest forces me back into my sweat-soaked mattress — pushes my sternum down to kiss my spine — slowly forces the air from me like when that Staffy would clamp down on its rubber bone (eyeballing you, daring you to try and take it) — whimpers/wheezes. As the knuckles of the toy rise up and meet on the brow of the pup's muzzle so my ribs converge above and envelope this fucker's foot.

Why did Channel 4 build their climactic set over my bed — is a sensible enough question but one that will have to wait as I'm struggling enough to raise my head from the pillow (I can smell the back of my head).

I may have gone too far

I collect the dust from hoover bags and bedroom window sills (I attempt to press diamonds from you between covers of your favourite books ((I stand on the neat pile, willing ever more pressure)) (((I think of all that weighed me down [before]))) ((((I hold 4 bags of sugar, 3 of potatoes, imagine 17 London buses stacked end-to-end)))) (((((I jump and twist [on the inane blurb] along to the latest dance craze))))) ((((((I remember that the Blue Whale is the largest creature to have ever lived and…hold…that…thought…)))))) (((((((I am being ridiculed by a Channel 5 camera crew as I'm lifted out of my [roofless] house))))))) ((((((((I am, as Bucky said, *going in* [there is no up or down])))))))) (((((((((I am Mr Motivator, power-squatting before breakfast))))))))).)   Today, I'm pressing diamonds from you.

(i) you said you don't know what I
am anymore / (eventually) I write
in a poem <3hrs & 36 mins later I
question why you said what instead
of who / but we're artists, right?
so I could take a stab at that one /
(but instead you said 'what' and
I don't know where to start)

'if you don't know what I am —
you who [quote/unquote] / you who
takes pictures of me as I sleep /
you who remembers me
in a way in which I never
existed) / you who said (or thought)
I was a good idea

(ii) between us I bought all the books with 'no' in the
title as if that would be our song, / 4 bare MDF shelves
(spotted by eagle-eyed friends on Tumblr) / we promised the
be the pricks that pushed the spines toward the wall

never to

(iii) and then there's this
issue of me not liking
this new keringan coffee /
and what even am I /
anywhere without the
funny / and I'm not
drink / and the promised
has changed since the
last time / and the green
summer / will be gone soon
(about fuck) / and
there are only so many
times you can blame
yourself

Q: Favourite kiss?
A: Under an umbrella.
for Anna K.

Love Umbrella,
barbed prongs fish for lover's eyes.
Favourite kiss? Hooked.*

*The noise escapes the coach house, in spurts, as if drawn along one of those clothes lines you've seen in old photographs of New York apartment buildings in the '50s (though, you're probably too busy wondering if they really did hang babies ((in baskets)) out of windows). Hunched over her work her torso bobs in time with the (off-centre) drive plate. Steel skims whetstone. (Precision ground.) Inside, cones of daylight creep through holes in lapped weatherboard (map out ((rough-edged)) ellipses on compacted soil). The small mound of filings gathering under the wheel (negatives of hundreds of hooks**). Satisfied with the honed point she fixes the hook to the rib of a black umbrella (curved mahogany handle) —

Unaware of their utter predictability, thousands of tourists funnel through *the main shopping street,* convinced of the randomness of their actions. (She watches from subterranean stairwells. ((Umbrella rests against tense thigh.)) (((Eyes level with brogues and pump.))) ((((Sprung-loaded mechanism snaps into action.)))) (((((Within four steps the familiar tug, the same yelp.))))) ((((((No time to look back)))))) (((((((On. Tug. Yelp.))))))) ((((((((Human mobile in hand. The struggling never lasting *too* long)))))))) (((((((((The pain of steel piercing flesh focuses the minds of the pair before the sudden, overwhelming realisation that *this* person. *This* dangling body, spinning slowly. *This* is their soulmate.))))))))) ((((((((((They pull each other closer. In. Barbed steel threatening to wrench white meat from bloodied sockets.)))))))))) (((((((((((The distortion of the retina always at its most beautiful before it tears.))))))))))) They kiss for the first time).

**4. We renounce, in sculpture, the mass as a sculptural element.

It is known to every engineer that the static forces of a solid body and its material strength do not depend on the quantity of mass... example a rail, a T-beam etc.

But you sculptors of all shades and directions, you still adhere to the age-old prejudice that you cannot free the volume of mass. — *The Realistic Manifesto,* Naum Gabo, August 5th 1920.

Yonkers

From that noose Tyler hangs in silhouette and it's had millions of views on YouTube. (You've contributed several hundred (and you took the image for yourself).) An acceptance that there is no original expression anymore is all well and good but it's only ethically sound when it comes with an *explicit* acknowledgement of the source (why notice the connection now? (Fraud.)).

Original interpretations? A series of binary responses. You *do* or you *do not*... *Acting up* in Dalston basements.

You can drown in a couple of inches of water (if only (but these puddles would never offer an escape (and that deluge will never cleanse (and all you want is to feel clean)))). Tyler's feet kick as the noose tightens and it's all for show. Fraud.

We analyse *the process* and we hold our heads up high because we've found a way to avoid taking responsibility for the outcome. Down the pub they'd (rightly) call you a 'jumped-up-prick' but a red velvet curtain has been drawn over that mirror and it's all been engineered in a way that allows you to avoid accepting your responsibility.

No one seems to have noticed the lie we've been sold. We're all soloists but we're not allowed to leave the orchestra pit.

Tyler's feet stop kicking (but he'll never die as long as the cursor remains over the play button (and you keep your head down (and focus on *the process* (and never face the mirror.)))). Fraud.

Du finner meg aldri igjen
for eg har gått av stien

I've lost everyone so far. But you had your net. *Followed with.* I had never so much tried to cover my tracks, as stamp all over the fucking place. And you scooped me up when I was at my lowest point. (Everything before you was below freezing.) Who'd have thought that your delicate fingers would hold as I bolted (again)(and again).

> In the vacuum between Christmas and New Year's I bond with the future father-in-law watching black and white footage of war planes refuelling. I quickly discard the idea of using trailing fuel lines as a metaphor for our connection. I've already binned more incomplete drafts addressed to you than any other *finished* shit intended as tribute to anyone else.

My default mode is escape. A pharmacist at the Maudsley advised me to look for an adrenaline inhibitor when considering a new course of medication. Though, running away isn't necessarily the same as disappearing. Just let a little line off the reel. Something to follow home. Fight ~~or~~ flight.

> I complain constantly that poets don't look at the world properly but I'm a hypocrite and no longer glance out of windows. (I trace endless hotel corridors. Run, forever, through that horror-movie-set looking for you.) Blinkered, over bridges. People misattribute vertigo but it's not a fear of falling — it's a fear of wanting to jump. *Escape.*

All I've ever seen in people's eyes is fear. Not that we're all permanently scared, rather it's the only emotion that exposes itself in our eyes. Friends — or writers, so perhaps not friends — talk of

62

how the act of writing captures and tames their fears. I dream of pushing all of my fear into these wet gobstoppers and digging them out with a hot teaspoon. I seem to remember, though I won't bother to Google it, that digging out your eyes wouldn't be painful. I'll use a hot spoon to increase the sensation in the socket behind the offending little shits. *Reassurance.*

> I've been told that the clearest sign of mental distress is a *dead* look in the eyes. They've always betrayed me. Given me up. I used to think that my distaste for looking at myself in the mirror was due to hating myself. It's always been more specific than that. These are not windows but peeling billboards advertising the very worst aspects of me.

But you clung on and I'll probably never understand why and you'll continue to hope I'll never look out of another window and we'll be married and we *will* be happy and the dead looks will come and go and we'll smile and I'll run and you'll hold on and it won't be as desperate as I *always* make it out to be but we will run blindly — or blinkered. Maybe that's the only way any of this shit is bearable?

it was *your* pocket it always was my
destination my goal cradled upward in your
permanently cold fingers deposited next to
the heat of your chest *home* i dreamt (years
ago) that enough of me would drain away
that i would shrink shrink down small
enough to be placed into your breast pocket
only you weren't you then that pocket wasn't
yours you said your regret was you'd never
told me how you really felt you're not alone
there i could never find the words to explain
how

Notes on the text

p.1   — The names in 'John Dickson' have been changed to respect people's privacy.

p.22   — Erik Pirolt is a painter, sculptor and film-maker from Kristiansand in southern Norway. 'String-section', 'Sounding' and 'Kerf' are all responses to individual paintings. www.pirolt.org

p.27   — 'Phosphate of Calcium' was written in response to a quote by John Berger — 'what reconciles me to my own death more than anything else is the image of a place: a place where your bones and mine are buried, thrown, uncovered, together. They are strewn there pell-mell. One of your ribs leans against my skull. A metacarpal of my left hand lies inside your pelvis. (Against my broken ribs your breast like a flower.) The hundred bones of our feet are scattered like gravel. It is strange that this image of our proximity, concerning as it does mere phosphate of calcium, should bestow a sense of peace. Yet it does. With you I can imagine a place where to be phosphate of calcium is enough.' — I was reluctant to include the full quote because, as you can see, it is far better than anything I've written in this book.

p.44   — 'Rim' was written after a prompt from exercise #3 in *52, Write a poem a week* (Nine Arches Press, 2015). I didn't get any further than this exercise.

p.53   — *The Dizziness of Freedom* is an anthology of poetry about writers' experiences of their mental health published by Bad Betty Press (2018).

p.62 — *Du finner meg aldri igjen for eg har gått av stien* is a lyric from 'Die Polizei' by Norwegian band Kaizers Orchestra.

Acknowledgements

Firstly, thank you to Paul and Sarer at Hesterglock Press for offering to publish this book and allowing me to do exactly as I wanted.

Thank you also to Arts Council England for their generous support of this project which allowed me to work with the amazing Eley Williams whose advice during the editing of the manuscript has been invaluable.

I definitely also need to mention Tom Bland (then editing the *Blue of Noon* blog) and Paul McMenemy (*Lunar Poetry Magazine*) for being the first people to publish any of my writing back in 2014, and for pushing me to send more.

Thank you to Abi Palmer, Anna Kahn, Astra Papachristodoulou, Emily Harrison, Melissa Lee-Houghton, Stephen Lightbown and Thomas Darby for reading through these and many other 'poems'.

Thank you to Isabel Waidner, Linda Boström Knausgård and Lydia Davis for giving me something to aspire to.

Sarah Sanders you are a star!

To all former guests of Lunar Poetry Podcasts — the hundreds of conversations I've been part of or edited is probably what led to this book (so you can blame them!).

To all the staff on the John Dickson ward at the Maudsley Hospital, in the spring of 2014, thank you for encouraging me to write again.

And to my boy-wife Lizzy — everything.

Hesterglock Press has a Patreon page.

Patreon enables a regular pledge of your choice to artists, writers, musicians etc in return for special rewards & exclusives. Patreon's platform allows working class artists like those behind Hesterglock Press to receive a steady revenue stream directly in contact with our readers. By signing-up and supporting us working in this way, you'll be helping to sustain an ongoing commitment to connecting with others, publishing radical & challenging books, collaborating with other artists and writers on projects that take-risks & don't / won't make a million, but may make a difference or a change.
Please support our publishing in return for free things like books, exclusive artworks and digital goodies. Take a look here https:// www.patreon.com/hesterglock
 - Paul Hawkins Bristol, UK (2019)

Forthcoming Hesterglock Press books:

[un].holy : 33 sonnets for Brigid - Sally-Shakti Willow
This Is the Way the World Ends - Pedro Eiras
WRITING UTOPIA - co-eds. Sally-Shakti Willow & Sarer Scotthorne
Soft Rich Digital Ghosts; tweeting carparks dry - SJ Fowler
Sealed - Andrew Wells
Monument - Louis Armand & John Kinsella
Place Waste Dissent (2nd edition) - Paul Hawkins
clew (2nd edition) - Lucy Furlong
The Blood House (2nd edition) - Sarer Scotthorne
Blue - Vik Shirley
The Poetarium - Miggy Angel

We will also be publishing new books by Sarer Scotthorne, SJ Fowler (in collaboration with The Aleph) and a graphic novel by Steve Ryan & Paul Hawkins

Lightning Source UK Ltd.
Milton Keynes UK
UKHW020824030120
356306UK00006B/30/P

9 781916 159464